Coping Effectively With Spinal Cord Injuries

Coping Effectively With Spinal Cord Injuries

A GROUP PROGRAM

Therapist Guide

Paul Kennedy

OXFORD
UNIVERSITY PRESS

2009

OXFORD
UNIVERSITY PRESS

Oxford University Press, Inc., publishes works that further
Oxford University's objective of excellence
in research, scholarship, and education.

Oxford   New York
Auckland   Cape Town   Dar es Salaam   Hong Kong   Karachi
Kuala Lumpur   Madrid   Melbourne   Mexico City   Nairobi
New Delhi   Shanghai   Taipei   Toronto

With offices in
Argentina   Austria   Brazil   Chile   Czech Republic   France   Greece
Guatemala   Hungary   Italy   Japan   Poland   Portugal   Singapore
South Korea   Switzerland   Thailand   Turkey   Ukraine   Vietnam

Published by Oxford University Press, Inc.
198 Madison Avenue, New York, New York 10016

www.oup.com

Oxford is a registered trademark of Oxford University Press

Library of Congress Cataloging-in-Publication Data

Kennedy, Paul, 1959–
Coping effectively with spinal cord injury : a group program : therapist guide / Paul Kennedy.
    p.   ;   cm. — (Treatments That Work)
Includes bibliographical references.
ISBN 978-0-19-533972-7 (paper : alk. paper)
1. Spinal cord—Wounds and injuries—Psychological aspects.   2. Spinal cord—Wounds and injuries—Treatment.
3. Group psychotherapy.   4. Stress management.   I. Title.   II. Series: Treatments that work.
[DNLM: 1. Spinal Cord Injuries—therapy.   2. Adaptation, Psychological.   3. Psychotherapy, Group—methods.
4. Spinal Cord Injuries—psychology. WL 400 K36c 2009]
RD594.3.K46 2009
617.4′82044—dc22

                                                                        2008026395

9 8 7 6 5 4 3 2 1

Printed in the United States of America
on acid-free paper

About Treatments *ThatWork*™

Stunning developments in healthcare have taken place over the last several years, but many of our widely accepted interventions and strategies in mental health and behavioral medicine have been brought into question by research evidence as not only lacking benefit, but perhaps, inducing harm. Other strategies have been proven effective using the best current standards of evidence, resulting in broad-based recommendations to make these practices more available to the public. Several recent developments are behind this revolution. First, we have arrived at a much deeper understanding of pathology, both psychological and physical, which has led to the development of new, more precisely targeted interventions. Second, our research methodologies have improved substantially, such that we have reduced threats to internal and external validity, making the outcomes more directly applicable to clinical situations. Third, governments around the world and healthcare systems and policymakers have decided that the quality of care should improve, that it should be evidence based, and that it is in the public's interest to ensure that this happens (Barlow, 2004; Institute of Medicine, 2001).

Of course, the major stumbling block for clinicians everywhere is the accessibility of newly developed evidence-based psychological interventions. Workshops and books can go only so far in acquainting responsible and conscientious practitioners with the latest behavioral healthcare practices and their applicability to individual patients. This new series, Treatments *ThatWork*™, is devoted to communicating these exciting new interventions to clinicians on the frontlines of practice.

The manuals and workbooks in this series contain step-by-step detailed procedures for assessing and treating specific problems and diagnoses. But this series also goes beyond the books and manuals by providing ancillary materials that will approximate the supervisory process in assisting practitioners in the implementation of these procedures in their practice.

In our emerging healthcare system, the growing consensus is that evidence-based practice offers the most responsible course of action for the mental health professional. All behavioral healthcare clinicians deeply desire to provide the best possible care for their patients. In this series, our aim is to close the dissemination and information gap and make that possible.

This therapist guide describes a time-limited group program designed to help individuals who have suffered a spinal cord injury (SCI). Participants in this program are taught various adaptive coping skills that they can use to manage stress and difficult situations. Over the course of seven sessions, participants learn problem-solving methods, ways of challenging negative thoughts, how to set up a system of social support, and relaxation exercises to help combat anxiety. They are taught the importance and benefit of being assertive and ways of effectively dealing with those individuals who may not understand their disability. The primary goals of this program are to increase people's capacity to cope and to increase their belief in their ability to manage their situation.

Complete with step-by-step instructions for running sessions, as well as lists of materials needed, session outlines, and copies of forms necessary for treatment, this therapist guide provides you with all the information you need to help SCI sufferers reclaim their lives and look to the future with optimism.

David H. Barlow, Editor-in-Chief,
Treatments *ThatWork*™
Boston, MA

References

Barlow, D. H. (2004). Psychological treatments. *American Psychologist, 59,* 869–878.

Institute of Medicine. (2001). *Crossing the quality chasm: A new health system for the 21st century*. Washington, DC: National Academy Press.

Acknowledgment

I am very grateful for the contribution of Dr. Charles King with whom I first explored this intervention, and Dr. Jane Duff for her input. I would also like to thank all the participants who freely gave their time, insights, and experiences.

Contents

Chapter 1 | *Introductory Information for Therapists*

Background Information and Purpose of This Program

Spinal cord injury (SCI) is a major trauma that has an impact on many aspects of a person's life. People with SCI will face challenges that they have not previously experienced. If the demands of these unfamiliar situations are perceived to be greater than the resources available to deal with them, then the person in that situation will feel stressed.

In major traumas such as SCI, the demands presented can be excessive and prolonged. This can result in levels of stress getting so high that they actually interfere with the person's ability to deal with the situation. Consequently, the situation gets worse, resulting in more stress. When this happens, it reduces people's confidence in their ability to cope and subsequently results in feelings of helplessness and poor self-esteem.

Coping Effectiveness Training (CET) consists of a series of group learning sessions aimed at helping people deal with the demands of SCI. It encourages people to think about the stressful situations that they experience following SCI and find ways of dealing with problems effectively so that stress reactions can be avoided. Through the process of dealing with each stressful situation, one at a time, CET builds people's confidence in their ability to cope and makes the results of SCI more manageable. Its main aims are to:

- improve skills for assessing stress

- teach a range of coping skills that can be used to tackle stress

- provide an opportunity for interaction with other people who have had similar experiences of SCI

The skills taught in this seven-session group treatment program have been developed from research and have proven effective not only for people with SCI but also for those who have experienced other types of injury or trauma. CET is designed to increase people's capacity to cope and to increase their belief in their ability to manage their situation.

Problem Focus

Most people with SCI are male (80%), under 50, and have acquired their injury as a result of a motor vehicle accident, fall, trauma, or medical incident. By the time they have reached the rehabilitation center, they will have some understanding of their prognosis and will be building an awareness of their new needs. In addition to the impairment of bladder, bowel, and sexual functions, they will need to consider their relationships, responsibilities, employment, recreation, and accommodation. Previous vulnerabilities, limited exposure to disability, and prevailing negative attitudes in society may impair their capacity for coping and mastery. People experience a range of emotions that includes anxiety, depression, anger, and frustration. Kennedy and Rogers (2000) found that between a quarter and one third of people with SCI experience significant depression in the first 2 years post injury. Rehabilitation can provide practical problem-focused solutions to some of these difficulties, and support from key professionals can help individuals build up a sense of adjustment and control. Rehabilitation also provides essential training to prevent complications and secondary problems such as pressure sores, substance misuse, and disengagement.

Development of This Treatment Program and Evidence Base

Using the cognitive theory of stress and coping as devised by Lazarus and Folkman (1984), King and Kennedy (1999) developed a CET program for use in SCI. A controlled trial comparing 19 patients receiving CET with 19 matched controls, using outcome measures of depression, anxiety, and coping, was carried out. Results indicated that participants in the intervention group showed significantly greater reductions in levels of depression and anxiety when compared with controls immediately after the intervention and at 6-weeks follow-up. However, no significantly greater change in the coping strategies used by the intervention group was identified. In an interview evaluation of the group, participants suggested that interacting with other group members was the most helpful aspect of the program.

The coping strategies people mobilize in response to the consequences of an SCI are important in determining the extent of the psychological distress experienced. There is a growing body of evidence which highlights the strong predictive relationship between the coping strategies utilized and the level of psychological distress. Depression and anxiety are often the consequences of escape-avoidance strategies, while positive affective states are associated with coping strategies such as acceptance, positive reappraisal, and problem-solving (Kennedy et al., 2000; Martz, Livneh, Priebe, Wuermser, & Ottomanelli, 2005; Reidy, Caplan, & Shawaryn, 1991). Duff and Kennedy (2003) have developed an adjustment model post-SCI emphasizing the importance of considering pre-injury factors such as emotional history and previous vulnerabilities, as well as the beliefs that the individual has about disability and his capacity to cope. Through a process of primary and secondary appraisal, the individual will mobilize either approach-focused coping or avoidance-focused coping. Approach-focused coping will result in a sense of mastery, self-efficacy, and posttraumatic growth. Conversely, avoidance-focused coping can lead to anxiety, depression, self-neglect, and substance abuse problems. The selection of approach- or avoidance-focused strategies is influenced by the primary and secondary appraisal processes followed throughout the early stages of the injury.

Kennedy et al. (2000) identified a number of coping strategies that were associated with positive adjustment, which included accepting the reality of the injury having occurred, availability of high quality social support, the capacity to engage in positive reappraisal, and engagement in planned problem-solving. Maladaptive coping strategies associated with poor adjustment included behavioral and mental disengagement, alcohol and drug use ideation, denial, escape-avoidance coping strategies, focusing on and venting of emotions, and low social support. Cognitive-behavioral therapies are common psychological interventions for the management of a range of emotional disorders, including depression, anxiety, and adjustment disorders. Elliott and Kennedy (2004) in their evidenced-based review of the treatment of depression, found that coping effectiveness training (Kennedy, Duff, Evans and Beedie; 2003) was the only published study to document significant effects of a psychological intervention for individuals with SCI in comparison with persons receiving no such treatment. SCIs result in many new situations that precipitate considerable uncertainty and fear about the future. If the individual has a belief that a situation can be managed, he is more likely to adopt a problem-focused strategy, which facilitates coping and adjustment. Individuals who appraise their SCI to be unmanageable have a low expectation of coping, which may impair adaptation. Tirch and Radnitz (2000) suggest six categories of cognitive distortions following SCI. These include: (1) an overly negative view of the self and others; (2) negative appraisals about self-worth following injury; (3) expectations of rejection from others and inadequacy; (4) the expectation about consistent failure; (5) development of excessive personal entitlement; and (6) an overdeveloped sense of vulnerability. Within cognitive-behavioral therapy (CBT), problems and issues are recast in forms amenable to solutions emphasizing hope and the expectation of success. Individuals are encouraged to monitor the relationships between thoughts, affect, and behavior, and to also evaluate the validity and viability of these associations. Challenging negative beliefs and replacing cognitive distortions with rational and realistic perspectives are also integral components in the therapeutic process.

Craig, Hancock, and Dickson (1999) advocate the provision of group-based CBT to ameliorate the emotional concerns of people with SCIs. They found, with the use of a non-randomized convenience control, that those who received a group-based CBT program during rehabilitation had significantly fewer hospital admissions and higher self-reported adjustment than non-randomly selected SCI controls. CET is generally based on the idea that coping has two functions: (1) to alter the problem causing a distress and (2) to regulate the emotional response to the problem. Once changeable aspects have been identified, the individual is trained to utilize problem-focused strategies. For those aspects that are unchangeable, the person is trained to utilize emotion-focused strategies.

Everyone at some point responds inappropriately to stress, which can exacerbate the situation. CET includes the identification of effective and ineffective responses to stress, especially those that are particularly unhelpful, such as disengagement, general avoidance, long-term denial, and the expression of extreme emotion. By encouraging individuals to think critically about their behavior in response to stressors, CET helps people avoid unproductive ways of coping. As mentioned, CET successfully reduced levels of depression and anxiety and also resulted in changes in negative self-perception and improved self-efficacy in coping with SCI. It was also effective in promoting and socially validating the belief that many aspects of SCI are indeed manageable. Kennedy, Duff, Evans, and Beedie (2003) evaluated a group-based CET program aimed at improving adjustment and enhancing adaptive coping post-SCI. In matched controlled trials with 85 participants, the intervention group showed a significant reduction in depression and anxiety although there was no evidence of change in the pattern of coping. Improvements were understood on the basis of change in participants' negative appraisals about the consequence of the injury and increased and socially validated (by peers) perception that the spinal cord injury is manageable.

Kennedy, Taylor, and Duff (2005) explored the characteristics of people who showed benefit from a group-based intervention aimed at improving psychological adjustment. Results from this study found that age, level of injury, gender, and coping strategies were not associated with treatment benefit; however, self-perception and time since injury were. This most likely captures the inherent dynamic nature of both coping and adjustment: neither are unitary events per se, but processes that unfold over time. The injured person's appraisals, emotional responses, and coping behaviors change and develop according to the change in situation during acute medical care, rehabilitation, and re-integration to the community.

The Role of Medications

The CET treatment is often provided in addition to individual adjustment and psychotherapy. Medications are often complex and the general tone is to encourage adherence.

Outline of This Treatment Program

CET aims to improve skills for assessing and managing stress, while providing participants with an opportunity for interaction with others who have similar experiences of SCI. The intervention consists of seven 90 min sessions run twice a week in groups of 8–12 people. The concept of stress is introduced in the first session and attempts are made to normalize stress reactions. The need to develop the ability to think critically about how one appraises and copes with situations is also emphasised. The second session covers appraisal skills and the third session, problem solving, which includes working through several reality-based scenarios commonly experienced by people with an SCI. In the fourth session, the connections and distinctions between thoughts, feelings, and behavior are examined with the inclusion of work on pleasant activity scheduling and relaxation. Session 5 is concerned with increasing awareness of negative assumptions, thoughts, and expectations and how to challenge them. The final two sessions describe the meta-strategy for choosing appropriate ways of coping and increasing social support. The provision of a meta-strategy for choosing the optimum coping response for a particular situation is important because research suggests that the effectiveness of individual coping strategies can vary at different times following an injury (Reidy & Caplan, 1994).

Use of the Participant Workbook

In addition to this guide, there is a corresponding workbook available for group members. The workbook contains psychoeducational information that participants can refer to in between sessions to reinforce what they learn in group. It also contains worksheets and forms for use during group exercises, as well as for completing at-home assignments. There is space throughout the workbook to record notes. Participants should be instructed to bring the workbook to every meeting.

Chapter 2 | *Group Logistics*

Forming a Group

This is perhaps the most important part of the process. Group members should be involved in active rehabilitation and represent a range of age, gender, and cultural groups. Thought should be given to the membership to include people with a variety of approaches and attitudes toward the disability. It is not helpful just to focus on those individuals who are most depressed or anxious. In order to create a well-balanced group, you will need a few individuals who have adjusted positively and coped well with their disability, as well as people with maturity and pre-injury resilience. People who have difficulty understanding the language used, have had a significant cognitive impairment, or have a mental health problem that may interfere with communication and reasoning may not find the group format helpful.

Group Size

The ideal size of the group is between 8 and 12 members. You may successfully run a group of six members, but not less than four. Even numbers are best as some in-group exercises require members to be split into pairs. For example, it is useful to begin the first session by having group members pair up and tell each other about themselves, including the details of their injuries, as well as their interests and any other information they'd like to share. Then, each pair of group members can introduce one another to the rest of the group.

Group Meetings and Program Duration

Make it clear to participants that you expect them to commit for the duration of the program. Ideally, groups should meet twice a week for a total of seven sessions, and sessions last no more than 90 min each. If it is difficult to hold meetings on a twice-weekly basis, you may schedule sessions once per week instead. It is never a good idea for the group to meet less than once per week, however. Some group members may wish to meet up on their own or maintain informal contact with other participants or the group leader outside of formal meetings. Encourage participants to keep in contact with one another through phone or email.

Generally the group is closed, meaning no new members are accepted after the program has started. Each session builds on the themes explored in the previous week. Sessions begin with a review of the previous meeting, as well as review of homework and participant progress.

Ground Rules

To run a successful group, it is important to establish ground rules and encourage all participants to adhere to them. Having rules keeps everyone on task and prevents the group from veering off course.

The most important rule is attendance. All participants should commit to attending all sessions and to showing up on time. If a group member is going to be late or cannot attend a meeting, she should contact the group leader prior to the start of the session.

Another important rule to establish is that of confidentiality. Successful groups respect the confidentiality of what is shared in group. What is said in the group stays in the group.

Because groups are about listening and talking, rules for participation also need to be set. Every group member should feel comfortable sharing with the rest of the group. Taking turns and being respectful of other members is an important rule and should be emphasized from the very start. If a particular group member is monopolizing the discussion, it is okay to tell that member to take a break. Then, allow someone else to speak. Some people need to hear others and learn how to stand back.

Honesty is another rule that should be established from the start. Encourage group members to be honest, open, and frank, as well as to have a sense of humor. Allow participants to express their views, while reminding them to keep an open mind. There may be times when participants disagree and it is during these times that it is important to remind members that differing viewpoints are valuable to the group because they enrich discussion.

Last but not least, let participants know that they are required to participate in group exercises and activities and complete all at-home assignments.

Troubleshooting

There are many issues that can arise when running a group program such as this. For example, you may have one participant who persistently interrupts others when they are talking. It is important to deal with this type of group member quickly and consistently. You may need to pull the member aside, either before or after a group meeting, and remind her of the rules of participation. Everyone in the group gets a turn to talk.

If someone dominates with severe negativity, you need to be able to take the lead and challenge the negativity directly. For example, if a group member says the best thing to do after an SCI is to commit suicide, you need to challenge this statement. Explain to the member, and the rest of the group, that statistics show that very few people with an SCI act on suicidal ideation. It can also be helpful to normalize thoughts of suicide by letting the group know that many people think about or consider suicide after a major trauma, but most individuals move on from this.

If your group has members who are shy and have trouble participating in group discussions, use humor and prompting to get them to talk. You may divide the group into pairs or smaller sub-groups so that non-participating members feel more comfortable sharing their thoughts.

The group leader or facilitator is responsible for running the sessions and guiding group discussions. It is helpful to plan each session ahead of time and make sure you have access to a variety of anecdotes and examples that you can use in sessions to facilitate discussion. Planning in advance is crucial for a successful group meeting.

Having a coleader can often be beneficial. If there are two facilitators, it is important that one be an experienced mental health professional. If working with a coleader, it is a good idea to have a short debriefing session at the conclusion of each group session, during which you can troubleshoot difficulties and issues that arose in the group and make a plan for managing them.

Chapter 3 | *Session 1—Introduction to Stress and Coping*

(Corresponds to chapter 2 of the workbook)

Materials Needed

- Flipchart or dry erase board and markers

Outline

- Provide overview of the program

- Make introductions

- Give practical information about group meetings

- Define stress and stress reactions

- Discuss stress as it relates to spinal cord injury

- Present the cognitive model of stress and coping

- Assign homework

Introduction to the Program

At the start of Session 1, provide an overview of Coping Effectiveness Training (CET). You may use the following sample dialogue:

> *CET is a group program aimed at helping people manage the demands resulting from spinal cord injury. Over the next several weeks, you will be encouraged to think about the stressful situations you have experienced following your injury and find ways of dealing with them effectively in order to reduce your stress. Part of the process of managing stressful situations is about deciding where to focus effort. It is overwhelming to look at all the changes and difficulties all at once.*

The goal of CET is to build up your confidence in your ability to cope with the injury and manage your life.

Group Introductions

Instruct group members to pair up and introduce themselves to one another. Each member should reveal three things about himself, such as where he is from, his age, whether or not he has any children, what he does for a living, etc. After group members have completed their interviews, ask one member of each pair to introduce the person he interviewed to the rest of the group. Take approximately 10 min for this exercise.

Practical Information

Let group members know that they will meet twice a week for a total of seven sessions. Members can record the program schedule in the space provided in the workbook. Because each session builds on the discussion of the previous one, it is important that everyone attends all sessions. Encourage group members to come to every meeting and to show up on time. Explain to the group that the success of the program depends on group participation, including talking and listening to others, as well as the promise of confidentiality. Whatever is said in the group stays in the group.

Take a few minutes to talk with group members about their reasons for attending the group and what they hope to achieve from the program.

Introduction to Stress

Engage the group in a discussion about stress. Explain that stress is a normal response to demanding situations. Everyone experiences stress from time to time. Although the word "stress" is often used in everyday terminology and seems simple, it actually represents a complex interaction of thoughts, feelings, and behavior.

You may use the following sample dialogue to facilitate further discussion:

Stress is a normal response to pressure and the demands of life. People usually respond well to such demands by flexible adaptation and by mobilizing effective ways of coping with pressure such as taking breaks from tasks, relaxing, watching TV, seeing friends, etc. However, problems may arise when demands are excessive or prolonged.

There are ways of managing the stresses of your injury. Part of the process of managing the situation is about deciding where to focus effort. There are a range of practical skills that you can use to tackle stress and its unpleasant effects. We will learn and practice these skills in group.

Stress Reactions

Stress reactions occur when stress is excessive or overwhelming. Such uncontrolled tension can reduce an individual's ability to enjoy life and place them at risk for depression and anxiety, as well as physical disorders. Review the following list of possible stress reactions with the group:

- Low mood

- Negative thinking

- Poor sleep

- Muscular tension

- General fatigue

Ask group members to pair up and talk about their own reactions to stress. Emphasize that although stress can sometimes feel overwhelming, there are always ways to manage it, even after a major event or trauma.

Stress and Spinal Cord Injury

SCI is a major trauma that impacts many aspects of a person's life. Following SCI, people face challenges that they have not previously experienced. Talk to the group about the stress caused by their injuries.

*Because SCI is new to you, initially it can be very demanding. You
will need to learn to cope with a variety of new situations. It is
important to manage stress effectively, otherwise you may become
overwhelmed and the stress will interfere with your ability to deal with
certain situations. The particular situation will only get worse then,
and you will experience even more stress.*

Discuss with the group the different types of stress triggers. First, there
are *external* factors, which are those situations or events that cause stress.
Examples of external factors include:

■ Anatomical changes that are difficult to discuss

■ The impact of the SCI on the family

■ Physical changes

■ Physical pain resulting from the injury

■ Requiring more time than before to complete tasks

■ Irritation with self or with others

In addition to external factors, internal factors can also trigger stress.
Internal factors are the thoughts and interpretations the individual
makes about external factors. Explain to the group that people interpret
a situation according to past experience and the relative importance of
the situation to them. Some individuals with an SCI may be concerned
that they will not be able to manage in the future, while others may
regard the future following the injury as a challenge to be overcome.

Encourage group members to list *external* and *internal* factors that can
lead to stress. Record responses on the flipchart.

What Influences Stress?

Continue the preceding discussion and talk about how thoughts about a
particular situation can influence whether or not a person perceives the
experience as stressful. Provide the group with the following examples:

*Think about receiving a promotion at work. Some people see a
promotion as an exciting challenge, whereas others may be afraid of
taking on a senior position. They may become extremely anxious about*

the prospect of having more responsibility and find it difficult to live up to someone else's expectations of them.

The same can be said of retirement. For some, retirement may be a chance to do all the things they never had time to do while they were working. Others may become depressed, however, because they can't do the job they loved anymore and they miss their colleagues.

Cognitive Theory of Stress and Coping

The cognitive model of stress proposes that by thinking about the ways in which a person deals with stress, he is able to improve the skills necessary for effective coping. You may use the following sample dialogue to facilitate discussion:

We have talked a bit about stress and what it is. It seems that there are two factors that determine how people deal with stressful situations. We all go through these two processes even though we might not know it on a conscious level.

The first process is appraisal.

Define appraisal for the group as the individual's personal evaluation of a stressful situation. It is what the person makes of the situation or experience. Does he view the situation as a challenge or a threat? How does the situation relate to him? Is it important or not?

The second process is coping.

Define coping for the group as a review of the coping strategies that people have and their belief in their own ability to manage the situation. What skills does the person have and which ones work the best? Examples of coping skills include:

■ Relaxing

■ Going out with friends

■ Exercising

■ Reading

■ Watching TV

It is important to note that not all coping strategies are useful. When a person copes well, the way he thinks about the situation and what he does about it match up. The result of good or *adaptive* coping is decreased levels of stress and a greater sense of control over the situation. When coping poorly, thoughts about the situation and the actions taken are in conflict. The result of poor or *maladaptive* coping is an increase in stress-related symptoms.

Closing the Session

End today's session by asking group members for their feedback and whether they have any questions about the material presented. Then, assign homework.

Homework

 Ask group members to think about their personal signs of stress and record them on the My Signs of Stress worksheet in the workbook.

Chapter 4   *Session 2—Assessing and Managing Stress*

(Corresponds to chapter 3 of the workbook)

Materials Needed

- Flipchart or dry erase board and markers
- Participants' completed My Signs of Stress worksheets

Outline

- Review previous session and homework
- Begin appraisal skills training
- Teach the group how to break down complex stressors into manageable parts
- Introduce the concept of coping
- Define adaptive coping
- Assign homework

Review of Previous Session and Homework

Remind the group of last week's discussion about appraisal and coping. Appraisal is what a person makes of the situation and coping is what the person does.

Review group members' completed My Signs of Stress worksheets and discuss.

Training in Appraisal Skills

Last week the group was introduced to the concepts of appraisal and coping. Today the group will learn how to effectively appraise stressful situations.

It is very important for individuals with SCI to identify exactly what is causing them to feel stressed. The first signs of stress are often emotional reactions and can include feelings of sadness, anger, fear, or anxiety. These emotions are normal as SCI causes a number of critical life changes and difficulties. Ask group members for examples of situations or experiences that make them feel these emotions. Tell the group that

> *Emotional reactions are normal. They are the first signs that you could get stressed unless appropriate coping skills are employed. Whenever you feel these emotions, it should trigger you to search for the causes of stress; to appraise the situation.*

Breaking Down Complex Stressors

SCI is a complex stressor that has brought about major changes in group members' lives. If they try to look at the injury as a whole, it can often seem too big and overwhelming to take it in at once. Explain to the group the importance of breaking this "global issue" down into a number of smaller, more specific issues.

> *It is important to break down your injury into the specific parts that cause you stress. In doing so, it is helpful to ask yourself the following questions:*
>
> *1. Who is involved?*
> *2. What is the situation/context?*
> *3. Where are these situations likely to occur?*
> *4. When did they last occur and are they likely to occur again?*
>
> *If you notice, I did not mention the "Why?" question. The question of why can lead to speculation and not to the task at hand. It is best not to ask yourself, why me? Why now? Etc. "Why?" questions aren't helpful.*

Illustrate this process by using the following example. You may write out the example on the flipchart. Alternatively, participants can follow along using the same example in the workbook.

Glenn is an SCI patient in the hospital. He sometimes needs assistance from the hospital staff, but oftentimes they ignore him.

Who is involved?	The staff on the ward.
What is the situation/context?	When I need some help with certain things, the staff claims they are too busy. They seem to make time for everyone else, however. I feel like they are ignoring me.
Where are these situations likely to occur?	On the ward mostly, when I need help with something.
When did they last occur?	This morning when I needed some help washing, and at dinner time when I needed assistance.
When are they likely to occur again?	It is most likely to happen in the morning and at mealtimes.

Breaking down the global stressor helps the patient to identify coping strategies that will help her manage effectively. The more detailed the description of the stressful situation, the easier it will be to establish the goals of coping and the more likely it is that the more appropriate strategy will be chosen. Explain to the group that

Getting a detailed concrete description makes it easier to start thinking about what needs to happen to cope better. It means you will be more able to make clear decisions about how to bring the situation back into your control and make it more manageable.

Ask each group member to break down an aspect of SCI into concrete situations that cause them stress. Members should notice that by asking questions, the situation becomes less overwhelming and they are better able to come up with possible solutions for relieving the stress it causes.

Coping Realistically

Coping refers to what an individual can actually think or do in response to a stressor. Explain the two major functions of coping to the group:

1. To help the individual manage or alter the problems that are causing the stress

2. To help the individual deal with her emotional responses to the problem

As discussed earlier, in order to cope effectively, a detailed description of the stressful situation is needed. This makes it easier to establish goals of coping and leads to better decisions about how to cope. Emotional responses are fundamental. Discuss this with the group:

> *The way you respond emotionally to a stressful situation is very important and can influence both how you appraise the situation and your decision-making process. Part of understanding your emotional reactions to events is to consider what they represent for you. For example, do they represent loss or harm, a possible threat, or a challenge/opportunity for growth?*

Ask group members to think of some examples of emotional reactions to situations as a result of the injury.

Types of Coping

Coping is about what can be changed, either in the problem itself or in the person's reaction to it. Define the two types of coping.

1. Problem-focused coping—managing or resolving the problems that are causing stress

2. Emotion-focused coping—changing emotional reactions to the problems

Problem-Focused Coping

Stress to group members the importance of recognizing exactly what aspects of a problem can be changed.

In this situation, it is helpful to ask the following questions:

1. *What are the external aspects of this specific situation that can be changed?*
2. *What elements of the problem are amenable to change?*
3. *Is it possible to change or manage in a different way your behavior or your actions toward who, what, where, and when?*

Let us apply this technique to the case of Glenn, the patient who believed he was being ignored by the hospital staff.

You may write out the following example on the flipchart or have participants follow along using the same example in the workbook.

What are the external aspects of this specific situation that can be changed?	The staff's behavior My behavior
What elements of the problem are amenable to change?	The staff could be more understanding I could change the way I ask for help I could change the way I react to not getting help
Is it possible to change or manage in a different way your behavior or your actions toward who, what, where, and when?	I will be more assertive with staff when I need help I will also arrange a time for them to see me in the morning and at dinner

Of course, there is always the possibility that a person might think, "Nothing can be changed." In certain cases, it may be possible to change the situation by challenging the negative thinking. For example, an individual who has recently sustained a complete cervical lesion may regard mobility in terms of walking and running. In this case, nothing about the situation can be changed. However, if the patient thinks of mobility in terms of getting from point A to point B, she can use other means such as a wheelchair, car, train, or airplane. Although the patient must acknowledge some loss, she has not lost all mobility and is able to change the situation.

Emotion-Focused Coping

There are many occasions when it is really not possible to change external aspects of the problem. In these situations, losses may need to be accepted. Ask the group for examples of losses related to their injury that cannot be changed (e.g., loss of mobility, loss of ability to participate in certain activities, or loss of friends who don't understand the disability). Regardless of the type of loss, the goal of coping remains the same. Explain to the group:

> *Certain situations may require an initial acceptance of things that can't be changed but also require an attempt at reducing distress by changing emotional reactions to the situation. This can be done by changing approach, attitude, and thoughts, and by addressing issues of acceptance. Thus, the emphasis is switched from problem-focused coping to emotion-focused coping.*

There are a number of losses associated with SCI, including the loss of mobility and the inability to engage in certain activities that the individual used to enjoy. In order for the person to progress, she must learn to accept these losses. It is important to note that acceptance is not about giving in to a loss but about accepting the reality of the loss so that the person is able to refocus her energy on new goals.

Adaptive Coping

Adaptive coping requires making an accurate appraisal of the stressor and then matching an appropriate coping strategy to that appraisal.

Explain to the group that if the matching is no good, coping will be ineffective. It is important to know in which situations it is better to use problem-focused coping and in which, emotion-focused coping.

When elements of a problem *can* be changed, patients should use problem-focused coping. This may include:

- problem solving

- active coping

- making decisions

- rehearsing solutions

- developing social and communication skills

In situations where change is *not* possible, patients should use emotion-focused coping. This may include:

- relaxation

- changing the way they think about the problem/situation

- reevaluating the significance of an issue

- changing the meaning of something for them

- using humor

Homework

 ✎ Ask participants to consider stressors related to SCI and identify those that can be changed or altered and those that are unchangeable using the Changeability Chart in the workbook.

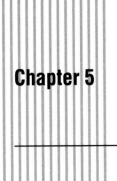

Chapter 5 | *Session 3—Problem Solving*

(Corresponds to chapter 4 of the workbook)

Materials Needed

- Flipchart or dry erase board and markers
- Participants' completed Changeability Charts
- Problem-Solving Worksheet

Outline

- Review previous session and homework
- Introduce problem-solving method
- Provide group with examples of problem solving
- Assign homework

Review of Previous Session and Homework

Last week the group talked about coping and how to use it to change either the problem itself or the person's emotional reaction to the problem. Remind the group that they have the power to change things; they are in control.

Review participants' completed Changeability Charts and ask them to share their perceptions of what sorts of issues were changeable and those that were not.

Problem Solving

Problem solving involves deciding which aspects of a problem are changeable. This is accomplished through working out the specifics of the problem (the who, what, where, and when) and figuring out which ones can be changed. Introduce the group to problem solving as follows:

Problem solving is a logical step-by-step procedure for coming up with practical ways of solving problems. Problem solving is used after you have appraised a situation and established which aspects of the problem are changeable.

Explain to the group the following steps of problem solving:

1. Identify the problem—specifically describe the aspects of the problem to be addressed

2. Identify the consequences of the problem—work on addressing the new needs and new consequences that have resulted from the injury

3. Generate possible solutions—all solutions should be explored, regardless of how silly or outrageous some of them may seem

4. Choose the best solution—evaluate each solution's advantages and disadvantages

5. Implement the solution—asking who, what, where, and when can be helpful here

6. Evaluate the success of the solution

To illustrate these steps, you may provide the group with examples. Two sample scenarios are provided here.

Case Example 1

Mary is being ignored by the waiter in a restaurant

Step 1: Identify the Problem

I am being ignored. My right to choose what I want is being denied. I am being treated as if I have no autonomy and as if I can't do anything. It's as if the waiter thinks I'm paralyzed in the head.

Step 2: What are the Consequences of the Problem?

I won't get my best choice and I'm certainly not getting good service. I am being made to feel less valuable and unintelligent. There is also a danger that the waiter's views will be confirmed.

Step 3: Generate Possible Solutions

I could be aggressive and tell the waiter to get a life. I could get upset. I could be submissive and just get by with it. Or, I could be assertive.

Step 4: Choose the Best Solution

If I'm aggressive, I'll end up getting worse service and I'll spoil dinner for myself and everyone else. If I'm submissive, I'll end up losing my self-respect. But if I'm assertive, I can get my choice, maintain my self-respect, and the other person will learn something.

Step 5: Determine to Implement the Solution

I will explain to the waiter that I would like to make my choices and will hold eye contact with him while I do this. I will act in control of the situation and will be polite without being submissive.

Step 6: Evaluate Your Success

The waiter was a little rude at first and did not make eye contact with me, but after a while he seemed to relax and was very friendly for the rest of the night. We all enjoyed dinner and I felt as if I had done something to help change the waiter's views.

Case Example 2

A person on the street is asked why he is in a wheelchair

Step 1: Identify the Problem

This is an intrusion of my privacy. This person only thinks of me as a disabled person and is ignoring the rest of me.

Step 2: What are the Consequences of the Problem?

I feel really disempowered and I also feel strange about being identified with a disability and not as myself.

Step 3: Generate Possible Solutions

I could get angry and tell her that it's none of her business. I could ignore her completely. I could laugh it off and explain the cause of my injury. I could explain to her that she's being rude in asking this question and that I'm a person, not a disability.

Step 4: Choose the Best Solution

I can't just block this out. I need to say something. If I get angry, I'll just make both of us upset. If I laugh it off then I'm being submissive and I'll disempower myself. But, if I explain to her that she's being rude and show her that I'm a person and not a disability, then I'll preserve my dignity and I'll be able to help her understand why she's being rude.

Step 5: Determine to Implement the Solution

I will politely tell her that she asked me a very rude question, and I will tell her that just because I am in a wheelchair it does not *make me a disability. I will also explain that she should not ask people that question in the future.*

Step 6: Evaluate Your Success

She was really shocked and seemed quite offended that I should take offense at what she had just asked me. I needed to challenge her views and I am glad that I did. I just hope that she is more tactful if she meets a person with a disability in the future.

Problem-Solving Scenarios

The sections that follow list different problem scenarios that group members may encounter as individuals with SCI. For homework, participants will use the Problem-Solving Worksheet in the workbook to apply the problem-solving method to each of these situations. If there is time in session, you may work with participants to problem solve several of these scenarios as practice.

Relationship Scenarios

- Your partner (wife, husband, boyfriend, girlfriend, etc.) seems nervous around you and afraid to touch you. What is going on? What do you do about it?

- Your partner (wife, husband, boyfriend, girlfriend, etc.) is visiting you in the hospital every night and neglecting all his or her other responsibilities and needs. You feel he or she should visit less. How do you handle this? What are some of the problems in this situation?

- Your family members are always trying to do everything for you. What do you do?

- What do you think you need to tell a future sex partner about your disability?

- Certain family members come to visit you every night and always leave you feeling lousy. How can you change this?

- Every time you mention sex, your partner seems nervous and changes the subject. What is happening?

- You have been dating someone for a while and wish to become sexually involved. How do you handle this situation?

- Your partner says he or she doesn't mind that you're in a wheelchair, but he or she doesn't kiss you goodnight when leaving. What's going on?

- A friend has invited you to a party and you are enjoying yourself there. Halfway through the party, you have a bladder accident. How do you feel? What do you do?

- You are single/unattached but are afraid of how others will react to you being in a wheelchair. How do you deal with this?

- You made holiday plans prior to your injury. Now you are at the treatment center and your partner/spouse wants to go without you. What do you do?

- You are out with your friends and all they talk about is sports and the activities they are involved in. How does this make you feel? What do you do?

- One of your best friends calls and keeps promising to visit but then he or she always has an excuse at the last minute. What's happening? What do you do?

- Your friends and family keep saying, "Work harder in physical therapy and you'll get better." What do you say or do?

Wheelchair-Access Situations

- You register for a class at the local university and the day you arrive you find out that the class has been moved to the second floor. There is no elevator. What do you do?

- You've gone to the movies with a friend (you've checked ahead of time that the theater is wheelchair accessible), but when you arrive, the manager insists that you sit at the very back beside the fire exit. How do you feel? What do you do?

- The store that you want to go into has a steep curb in front of it. What do you do?

- It's raining outside and you're at home. You need milk and other important items. What do you do?

- You are going for a job interview. You arrive at the company building and there is a flight of steps in front of you. What do you do?

- You go to see a movie and the usher at the theater tells you that no wheelchairs are allowed inside. What do you do?

- Your friends are having a party in a third-floor walk-up apartment in a building without elevators. What do you do when you receive the invitation?

Others' Reactions to Your Disability

- You are at a party and have met three new people. All have asked you why you are in a wheelchair. How do you answer them? How do you feel?

- You are sitting in the kitchen with your brother discussing what to buy for your mother's birthday. You ask him for a ride to the mall, but he insists on buying the present for you. What do you do?

- You are with a friend at a restaurant. The waiter asks your friend what *you* would like to eat. What do you do?

- You're putting the wheelchair into the car and a passerby insists on helping. What do you do?

- You are waiting in line at the bank and someone cuts in front of you. What do you do?

- You are out shopping and a person on the street is staring at you. What do you do?

- You are out when a small child runs up to you and asks, "What's wrong with you?" How do you respond?

- The child's mother runs up and drags the child away. What do you do now?

- You are seated at a table in a restaurant. After 20 min, no one has come to take your order. What do you do?

- You are confronted by three people on the street who try to rob you. What do you do?

- You come to an intersection in your wheelchair and a pedestrian grabs your chair to push you across the street. How do you react?

- Your employer comes to visit you in the hospital and "hints" at the possibility that you may not get your job back. What do you do?

Homework

✎ Have participants use the problem-solving method and the Problem-Solving Worksheet in the workbook to work through as many sample scenarios as they can.

✎ Remind participants to take note of which aspects of each particular problem are changeable and which ones are not.

Chapter 6 | *Session 4—Managing Emotions*

(Corresponds to chapter 5 of the workbook)

Materials Needed

- Flipchart or dry erase board and markers

- Participants' completed Problem-Solving Worksheets

- Pleasant Events Schedule

- Relaxation script

- Audiotape recorder and tapes to record relaxation script (optional)

Outline

- Review previous session and homework

- Present cognitive model of emotions

- Introduce pleasant activity scheduling as a way to combat negative thoughts

- Introduce autohypnotic relaxation technique

- Assign homework

Review of Previous Session and Homework

Last week the group discussed and practiced problem solving. For homework, participants were asked to apply the problem-solving method to various scenarios they are likely to encounter as individuals with SCI. Review participants' completed Problem-Solving Worksheets and discuss.

Emotional Reactions

SCI can bring about many emotions. Most people have a very normal emotional response to an SCI. They may feel depressed because of the losses they have experienced, feel anxious because of their fears and doubts about the future, or may feel angry and experience a sense of injustice. Ask group members if they have experienced any of these emotions.

Some of the emotions group members are feeling may be very new to them. They may also be very intense. Explain to the group that strong emotions are not a problem unless they are managed improperly. This leads to a discussion of negative thoughts and the cognitive model of emotions.

Cognitive Model of Emotions

When people feel depressed, they often have negative thoughts about themselves or the world in general. These thoughts lead to increased feelings of depression and further increase negative thoughts. This is called a "negative spiral" and is illustrated in Figure 6.1. Explain this to the group using the following sample dialogue:

> *Emotions don't just come out of the blue. They tend to be triggered by what we are thinking and what assumptions we make about ourselves, the world, and relationships. For example, if you are feeling vulnerable, you may be having gloomy or sad thoughts. These negative thoughts can make you feel even more vulnerable, creating a negative spiral.*

One of the major problems with this scenario is that people often focus on the emotions and not the negative thoughts. The purpose of today's session is to teach group members two ways of managing strong emotions that can lead to negative, unhelpful thoughts.

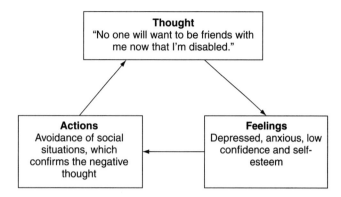

Figure 6.1

Negative Spiral of Thoughts, Feelings, and Actions

Pleasant Activities

When feeling low and depressed, individuals are less motivated to do things, especially pleasurable and interesting things. Reengaging in activities that bring pleasure is a good way to manage emotions. Discuss this with the group.

> *The less you get involved in pleasurable activities, the more you get caught up in negative thoughts and emotions and the more likely you are to remain depressed. However, knowing that there is a negative relationship between pleasant activities and depression gives you access to a powerful tool to control your mood. It is important to balance out unpleasant activities with pleasant ones.*

There are three types of pleasant activities. Review the following with the group:

1. Pleasant social activities

2. Competency activities (activities in which a goal is achieved, leading to a sense of competency)

3. Activities that are incompatible with emotional distress

Ask group members to provide examples for each category and record responses on the flipchart. Then, address the fact that engaging in pleasant activities may be especially hard when a person feels down or thinks that she can no longer do enjoyable things. The following three steps may help patients plan and introduce pleasant activities into their lives.

1. Decide what, when, how, and with whom

2. Set realistic goals

3. Commit yourself to doing it—and do it!

Scheduling Pleasant Activities

People are not born with certain interests; instead, interests develop through experiencing activities and developing competence. It is important to recognize how pleasant activities can have an impact on how the individual feels and to develop a plan for increasing the number of pleasant activities in her life.

A simple yet effective way of scheduling activities is for individuals to generate a list of pleasant activities through brainstorming. Ask each group member to generate a list of activities that she enjoys and is capable of doing. Patients can use the pleasant events schedule in the workbook for this exercise. A sample schedule is provided here.

Table 6.1 Sample Pleasant Events Schedule

Going to a rock concert	Planning trips or holidays	Going shopping
Doing art work	Going to a sporting event	Going to the races (car, boat, horse, etc.)
Breathing clean air	Writing or arranging a song	Setting goals
Thinking about something good in the future	Playing cards	Laughing
Solving a puzzle, crossword, word jumble, etc.	Having lunch with friends	Playing with pets
Learning a foreign language	Spending time with family	Taking a bubble bath
Playing a board game	Reading a book	Wearing a new outfit

continued

Sitting in the sun	Playing videogames	Meeting friends for a drink
Discussing religion or philosophy	Listening to the sounds of nature	Listening to the radio
Getting a massage	Writing letters or cards	Hearing and telling jokes
Lifting weights	Doing woodwork	Playing a musical instrument
Playing darts	Keeping a journal	Knitting, sewing, crocheting, etc.
Talking on the telephone	Going to a museum or exhibition	Going to the movies
Meditating	Reading magazines or newspapers	Going to the library
Taking a cooking class	Attending a play, opera, ballet, or concert	Traveling

Relaxation Training

Difficult situations cannot always be changed. In such cases, it is often helpful to try to change cognitive and emotional responses to those situations. Relaxation is a useful way of dealing with emotional reactions to difficult situations. It is an important skill for coping with tension and stress.

If you wish to practice autohypnotic relaxation during today's session, please use the following relaxation script. You may also audiotape the relaxation exercise for group members. Alternatively, group members can practice relaxation using the same script that is provided in the workbook.

Autohypnotic Relaxation Script

To start this relaxation process, we will concentrate first on your breathing. I want you now to concentrate on breathing. Breathe slowly in ... and slowly out. Deeply in . . . and deeply out. Not too vigorously, just deeply, gently breathe in . . . and out. The more you continue practicing this breathing, the more tension and discomfort you will breathe out. Concentrate on the feelings of relaxation and begin to allow yourself to let go, to relax. Notice how your body is slowly becoming very heavy and very comfortable.

Now I want you to fix your gaze on a spot in front of you. Try to find a spot on the wall or on the ceiling that you can concentrate on. Fix your eyes on that spot—concentrate—look at the spot. Try to resist blinking and imagine your eyes are connected by an imaginary line to the spot. Concentrate on the spot for a short while.

Meanwhile, continue to slowly breathe in . . . and slowly breathe out. Notice how comfortable it can be by allowing yourself to become more relaxed. Just allow yourself to become more relaxed. Concentrate on the spot and try to resist blinking. Notice that your eyes are becoming tired and a little heavier. Try to resist the temptation to blink. Breathe slowly in, and visualize your lungs filling with air and the air leaving your lungs totally when you breathe out.

You are beginning to regulate your breathing. Keep concentrating on the spot . . . your eyes are becoming very heavy and you are finding it difficult to keep them open. The spot is becoming hazier and you feel your eyes and your body becoming heavier. Now it is very difficult to keep your eyes open. Again, try to concentrate, try to resist blinking, but allow yourself to fall into a deeper state of relaxation. Your eyes are becoming very tired and very heavy. Imagine your lungs filling with air as you breathe in and the air leaving your lungs totally as you breathe out.

Close your eyes now and notice that feeling of heaviness. Your eyelids feel very heavy, and the heavier they become, the more relaxed you feel. Feel the relief in your eyes and encourage that relief and relaxation to spread from your eyes to the rest of your body. Continue to allow the feelings of heaviness and relaxation to spread, and allow yourself to fall into a deep level of relaxation and comfort, falling deeper and deeper through the three stages of comfort and relaxation.

In the first stage, I want you to let your body relax. I want you to think of your hands . . . now think of relaxing them, letting go. Think of your arms . . . relax them . . . let go. Allow them to become heavy. Now think of your shoulders . . . relax them . . . let go and relax. Now think of your feet . . . think about what they look like and think about them becoming relaxed by letting go of any tension and anxiety. Think of your legs, think of your lower legs, think of your thighs . . . let go . . . and relax. Breathe slowly in . . . and slowly out. Now think of your back, the lower back, the abdomen . . . and relax, let go, relax deeply. Again, remember to breathe slowly in . . . and slowly out. Think of the muscles in your upper back, your chest . . . relax . . . let go, breathing slowly in . . . and slowly out. Now, I want you to move on to the muscles around your neck. Think about them becoming very relaxed as you let go, more comfortable, your body becoming heavier. You are still breathing slowly in . . . and slowly out. Now think of the muscles in your head and on your face . . . now let go, and allow yourself to fall into a very deep state of relaxation.

Now you are passing through the first stage of relaxation. Discomfort and tension in your body fall away and you fall into a very deep state of relaxation. This relaxation enables your body to become very relaxed. You are becoming very heavy, sinking deeper and deeper into a comfortable state. Try not to resist these feelings, just allow them to happen.

Your body has become very relaxed and comfortable as you have completed the first stage.

If you have any discomfort, try and visualize this discomfort as a block of ice in a very warm room; the ice very slowly melts. At first we can't see it melting, but gradually the ice and the discomfort slowly fade away. Although you can't see the ice melting, you don't try to resist it and you allow yourself to fall deeper and deeper into the second stage of relaxation.

In the second stage, I want you now to think of your mind being relaxed. Think of letting go of any concerns or worries, things that are pushing themselves into your mind, thoughts that you feel need attention. I want you to let go of them and concentrate on being relaxed. Your body is relaxed, your body has become relaxed, and your body is becoming even more relaxed.

Now I want you to allow yourself to become relaxed in your thoughts. Your body is relaxed, and your body is becoming even more relaxed. Now I want you to concentrate on becoming more relaxed in your mind. If you have any concerns, just allow these concerns to become very light and allow them to float away. Put them to the side. You can come back to them, but now you have to let them go and relax. Imagine your mind becoming bigger and bigger, and this allows you to let go of any anxiety, worries, or concerns. Concentrate on the word "relaxation," what it means, then allow yourself to move through the second stage of relaxation.

I want you to visualize yourself entering the third and final stage of relaxation. In this third stage you are bringing your body and your mind together; bringing them together both very comfortable and very relaxed. You are comfortable. You have let go of your physical discomfort. You have let go of the physical tension. You have let go of the worries and concerns in your mind. You are going to allow yourself to fall deeper and deeper into a state of comfort and relaxation—breathing slowly in . . . and slowly out. Your body has become very heavy and your mind is becoming very clear. Let go of them together—mind and body.

Just concentrate on your breathing now, and this time when you breathe out, you are breathing out more of this discomfort, becoming more settled, much heavier, and just notice the sensation of becoming a little bit warmer, very slowly at first, but you are becoming warmer.

Now allow yourself to settle in this relaxed, comfortable, and heavy state. Your mind is clear and your body is heavy. Just allow yourself to enjoy these feelings, breathing slowly in . . . and slowly out. Imagine the tension continuing to drain from your body as you breathe out. Breathe in through your nose . . . and out through your mouth.

Establish yourself now on this pleasant pattern of breathing.

I now want you to use that clearness that is in your mind at the moment. Your body and mind together have moved you through the third stage. Your mind is clear, you have let go of the discomfort, of the tension and concerns. If they come through, just put them away, put them to the side, think of the clearness in your mind and how relaxed you have become.

Imagine yourself now . . . just imagine yourself moving into a different place. In your mind's eye imagine feeling very warm. Imagine going down a long passage into somewhere that is very safe. Just imagine yourself in a garden, the sun shining, and a gentle breeze. Just visualize being there. It doesn't matter how you feel, it doesn't matter what state you are in. Just imagine being there, with the sun shining and a gentle breeze.

There is a small wall around this garden. Inside this wall you are content and comfortable. Outside the wall . . . is outside the wall, and you want to let go of this for the moment. So just allow yourself to settle, comfortable and relaxed. Think through times when you were very content and happy. Just allow yourself to move through these thoughts, feelings, and places. You are now safe, settled, and relaxed. Imagine times when you were very content. Wander through these images, through these thoughts, and experience those feelings.

Just allow your mind to do this for a few moments.

Think of feelings of warmth, comfort, safeness, and heaviness.

Enjoy the feelings of relaxation.

Remember that you have created this relaxation, and the more you practice, the deeper, more comfortable, and more relaxed you will become.

Now I want you to think of becoming a little bit more alert. I want you to hold on to the relaxation. Hold on to that feeling. Hold on to the sense of safeness. I want you to imagine yourself now moving through the stages. You remain comfortable and relaxed, but a little bit more alert. When you become alert, you will think clearer, you will be relaxed and you will feel relaxed.

So I want you to move from the third stage through to the second stage. Again, you're comfortable, relaxed, and becoming more alert. Your mind is taking control again. Your mind is becoming clearer. You are becoming more awake.

I want you now to move into the second stage; your eyes slowly opening, becoming more awake, more alert.

Now into the first stage; you're becoming fully awake and fully alert. You have held onto the feelings of relaxation and comfort. You are fully awake and fully alert.

Homework

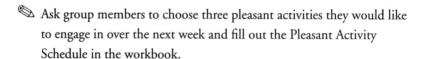 Ask group members to choose three pleasant activities they would like to engage in over the next week and fill out the Pleasant Activity Schedule in the workbook.

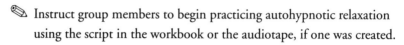 Instruct group members to begin practicing autohypnotic relaxation using the script in the workbook or the audiotape, if one was created.

Chapter 7 | *Session 5—Changing Negative Thinking*

(Corresponds to chapter 6 of the workbook)

Materials Needed

- Flipchart or dry erase board and markers

- Thought Record

Outline

- Review previous session and homework

- Discuss negative automatic thoughts and review common thinking errors

- Review steps for challenging negative thoughts

- Assign homework

Review of Previous Session and Homework

Last session, the group talked about the spiral of negative thinking and the things people can do to relieve intense emotions that can lead to unhelpful, negative thoughts, such as relaxation and participating in pleasurable activities.

Inquire about last week's task to begin engaging in pleasant activities. Ask group members what activities they tried and how they went about planning them and fitting them into their schedules. Also review participants' experience with relaxation.

Thoughts are very powerful in influencing mood and behavior. Explain to the group that

We all have some negative beliefs about ourselves and the world that encourage us to conclude that a situation is hopeless, when in fact we could do something about it.

These beliefs generate negative thoughts which influence our emotional reactions to events, often to a greater extent than the event itself.

Although people may not view their negative, unhelpful thoughts as being unrealistic, these thoughts often contain "thinking errors." Review the following common thinking errors with the group.

Overgeneralization. Taking one unfortunate situation and drawing sweeping, generalized conclusions from it.

Example: "My mother couldn't visit me today. She can't deal with seeing me like this."

Discounting the positive. Ignoring positive aspects and focusing only on the negative.

Example: "My physical therapist says I am making progress, but I still can't walk, so what does it matter?"

Black-and-white thinking. Thinking of things in absolute terms, like "always", "every," or "never".

Example: "I will never be able to work again."

Catastrophizing. Predicting the future negatively without considering other, more likely, outcomes.

Example: "I won't be able to run my house or take care of my children. My husband/wife will leave me and my kids will resent me, and my life will fall apart."

Personalization. Holding oneself personally responsible for an event that is not entirely under one's control.

Example: "If I hadn't gone shopping that day, I wouldn't have gotten in the accident and I wouldn't be in a wheelchair."

Jumping to conclusions. Assuming something negative where there is actually no evidence to support it. Two specific subtypes are also identified:

- *Mind reading*—Assuming the intentions of others. Arbitrarily concluding that someone is reacting negatively to you.
  Example: "My partner went to bed early. He no longer finds me attractive because I'm in a wheelchair."
- *Fortune telling*—Predicting future events will turn out badly despite the lack of evidence to support this.
  Example: "My friends won't invite me to their annual house party now that I'm disabled."

Emotional reasoning. Assessing a situation solely in emotional terms.

Example: "My parents are desperate for me to walk again. I'm letting them down."

Shoulds, musts, and oughts. Expecting that yourself or others should, must, or ought to be a certain way.

Example: "My friend should understand what I'm going through."

Explain to the group that negative, unhelpful thoughts can lower a person's mood. They can make someone feel depressed, scared, and demoralized. As briefly discussed last week, negative thoughts lead only to more negative thoughts, creating a negative, downward spiral.

Changing Negative Thoughts

The first step in changing negative thoughts is to learn to discriminate between realistic and irrational thinking. Be sure to stress to the group that this is not simply an issue of thinking positively but looking at how irrational thinking can be replaced by more realistic thinking.

To recognize unhelpful and negative thoughts, we need to deliberately think about what our thoughts are and look for what keeps these thoughts going.

One way to identify your negative thoughts is to notice the next time you feel low or scared and try to catch the thoughts that go through your head. Once you identify the thoughts, you can begin to challenge them.

The first step in challenging your negative thoughts is to ask yourself, what is the evidence that the thoughts are true? Then, explore the evidence for and against your thoughts. Ask yourself, am I making thinking errors? Would others accept these thoughts as true? Finally, come up with alternative, more rational thoughts. Ask yourself, what advice would I give to a friend who was having these types of thoughts? What explanation would be most helpful?

Refer group members to the list of SCI-related negative, automatic thoughts in the workbook. Ask them to consider each example and identify the common thinking errors represented. Have participants use the Thought Record in the workbook and follow the steps just described to replace the negative thoughts with more realistic ones. A copy of the list of negative thoughts is also provided here for your reference.

- "I won't be able to run the house now. I can't do anything."

- "My partner won't be able to cope with me being a burden. He will leave me."

- "I used to be a professional athlete. I've never had another job. I'll never be able to work again."

- "No one will want to be with me now that I'm disabled."

- "I'll never be able to look after myself. What's the point in carrying on?"

- "My hands don't work, my legs don't work, nothing works. I'm useless."

- "I can't look after my kids if I'm in a wheelchair."

- "With my level of injury, I'm always going to have to rely on other people, so what's the point of rehab? I may as well give up."

- "I'm not progressing fast enough with my rehab."

- "No one will find me attractive now."

Homework

 ✎ Ask group members to think about the relationship between strong emotions and thinking. When they experience strong emotions, they should use the Thought Record in the workbook to identify the thoughts that accompany these emotions and then replace them with more rational thoughts.

✎ Instruct group members to continue practicing autohypnotic relaxation and engaging in pleasurable activities.

Chapter 8 · *Session 6—Maladaptive/Adaptive Coping*

(Corresponds to chapter 7 of the workbook)

Materials Needed

- Flipchart or dry erase board and markers

Outline

- Review previous session and homework
- Review general information about stress, appraisal, and coping
- Revisit coping strategies
- Discuss maladaptive coping
- Assign homework

Review of Previous Session and Homework

Last session, the group discussed negative, automatic thoughts and how to go about changing them. Common thinking errors were reviewed and participants practiced challenging negative thoughts by evaluating the evidence for and against them.

Ask group members to give some examples of negative thoughts they experienced since the last session and talk about how they went about identifying and challenging them.

Review of Stress, Appraisal, and Coping

Today's session serves as a summary of the main themes the group has covered thus far. The group will review general information about stress and effective coping, as well as coping strategies.

Provide the group with a brief overview of stress, appraisal, and coping as follows:

> *As we discussed early on in the program, stress is a normal response to pressure and the demands of life. Normal levels of stress are manageable, but when stress is elevated, it becomes harder to handle. The first step in coping with stress is appraisal.*
>
> *Appraisal is the process of analyzing a stressful situation and evaluating whether it represents a threat or a challenge. This can be accomplished by breaking down the situation into its main components—namely, the who, the what, the where, and the when. This helps us determine our coping strategy. We did this in Session 2.*
>
> *Coping is the process of using available resources and skills to manage the stressful situation. Remember, we can either change the situation itself or our reaction to it.*

Review problem-focused coping and emotion-focused coping with the group (See Chapter 4 for more details.) Remind participants that adaptive coping is when a person's analysis of the situation and her coping strategy complement each other, resulting in a decreased level of stress and a feeling of being in control. Maladaptive coping has the opposite outcome. You will discuss maladaptive coping in more detail later on in the session.

Review of Coping Strategies

Discuss coping skills that are helpful, such as problem solving (useful for those stressful situations that are amenable to change) and relaxation and engaging in pleasurable activities (useful for those stressful situations that are more resistant to change).

Coping is a constantly changing process, and at certain times, some strategies work better than others. This is why individuals need to practice a range of coping strategies. Review with the group the following additional strategies that can help them cope with stress:

- Acceptance—accepting that they have an SCI and the consequences it brings to their lifestyle

- Positive reframing—looking at new ways of learning from the experience

- Active thinking and planning—figuring out the best ways to deal with certain situations

- Humor—telling jokes and laughing to help get through life's frustrations

- Prioritizing—focusing their limited resources on the issues that really matter to them

- Confrontation—confronting stressful situations and using problem solving

- Social support—seeking and receiving support from others

Remind group members that appraisal is the key to choosing the appropriate coping strategy for a particular stressful situation. If the situation changes, a new coping strategy may be needed.

Changes may occur because of the emergence of new information, the occurrence of new events, or a shift in a person's beliefs or perceptions. Explain to the group that when a change occurs, the situation needs to be reevaluated and a new coping strategy chosen.

Maladaptive Coping

As previously mentioned, maladaptive coping is when a person's appraisal of the situation and the coping strategy she chooses to use do not match up. Elaborate for the group:

> *There are many different ways to respond to stress. We have discussed some of the more effective strategies associated with stress management.*

However, if we engage in maladaptive strategies, they will result in poorly controlled stress, feeling more out of control, and the situation will not improve.

Ask the group to provide examples of unhelpful coping strategies that are likely to lead to increased levels of stress. Supplement their responses with the following:

- Doing nothing about the problem

- Avoiding thinking about their injury and what it means to them

- Denying that they have an injury and not doing the things they need to do (e.g., physical therapy)

- Expressing extreme emotion (e.g., constantly talking about how bad they feel)

- Thinking about using drugs or alcohol

Ask group members to think about a particular situation in which an unhelpful coping strategy may be used. Ask them to identify the strategy and consider some more helpful alternatives.

Homework

✎ Instruct group members to think about the coping strategies that they generally use and consider whether they are adaptive or maladaptive.

✎ Ask participants to think of one adaptive strategy that they can continue using and one maladaptive strategy that they can discontinue.

✎ Group members should continue practicing autohypnotic relaxation and engaging in pleasurable activities.

Chapter 9 | *Session 7—Social Support (Final Session)*

(Corresponds to chapter 8 of the workbook)

Materials Needed

- Flipchart or dry erase board and markers

Outline

- Review previous session and homework

- Discuss social skills and ways to deal with people without a disability

- Explain the importance of being assertive

- Introduce the concept of social support and the different types available

- Talk about ways of obtaining and maintaining social support

- End the program

Review of Previous Session and Homework

Last session served as a review of the major themes of the program, with a focus on maladaptive coping strategies.

Ask group members if they were able to identify any maladaptive coping strategies they may have been using and if they were able to discontinue them. What helpful or adaptive coping strategies were they able to increase?

Discuss with the group the importance of social skills and learning how to deal with people without a disability who often have problems understanding the concerns of people with a disability. You may use the following sample dialogue:

As a person with a spinal cord injury, you need to learn how to deal with people without a disability. They may have problems understanding what a spinal cord injury means and be unsure of how to relate to you. It is important that when you are faced with such people, you are able to deal with the ignorant views they may have and help to educate them.

Talk to the group about the most common ways of managing various situations they may encounter. Most people are aggressive, submissive, or assertive.

Aggression

When people behave aggressively it gives the message that others matter less than they do. Define aggressive behavior for the group as being prepared to harm others and being frequently rude, abusive, and sarcastic. Although people who behave aggressively might get what they want in the short term, persistent aggressive behavior can result in hostile reactions from others, social exclusion, and reprisal.

Submission

When people make submissive responses, they give the message that they do not matter or that other people's needs are more important than theirs are. Define submissive behavior for the group as requiring the repression of feelings, and explain that although it may avoid conflict, it can also end up making the person feel bad because his feelings are discounted.

Assertion

Someone who is being assertive communicates self-respect and a wish to have their own needs met, whilst according equal status to others. Define assertive behavior to the group as a person's ability to express how he feels and what he wants, as well as acknowledging that his own rights are as important as anybody else's.

Discuss with the group the aggressive, submissive, and assertive ways of dealing with the following situations:

- You are putting the wheelchair into the car and managing okay, but a passerby insists on helping

- Your caretaker keeps doing things that you are capable of doing yourself

- Your mother and her friend come to visit you. Rather than asking you, your mother's friend says to your mother, "Do you think he wants a drink?"

Have group members think through three different types of responses for each scenario and record them in the space provided in the workbook.

Assertive Rights

It is important that SCI patients learn to be assertive, especially when dealing with ignorant or biased individuals. Assertiveness can be confused with aggression, so it is important that patients are made aware that the key difference between the two is that assertiveness does not violate the rights of others. Assertiveness is about finding a situation in which all parties win. Review the following aspects of assertive behavior with the group. Assertiveness involves

- Developing the ability to express thoughts and feelings honestly

- Being open to taking risks

- Showing respect

- Being sensitive to others

- Being responsible for one's own behavior

Remind group members of the two examples of how to be assertive given in Session 3. By asserting their own rights and needs, each individual in the examples was able to achieve what he wanted from the situation.

The Importance of Social Support in Coping

Stress and coping generally take place within a social context involving other people. Explain to the group that

> Most people need social support and having and maintaining good, supportive relationships is helpful in managing your adjustment and coping with the future. We often take social support for granted and think of it as something that is either there or not. We need to learn how to choose and get the right kind of support and look after the support that we have.

Types of Social Support

There are different types of social support that serve different functions. You may use the following sample dialogue to facilitate discussion about the types of social support:

> We get practical support in the form of information and advice from a variety of people. We also get tangible support from close friends and relatives, and we get emotional support from people with whom we are very close.

> The appraisal process will help you understand the type of social support that will be helpful. Once you have identified the type of social support that you require in a particular situation, you will be able to identify the people in your social support network who are able to provide it.

Ask the group to give examples of the different types of social support. Record the responses on the flipchart.

Obtaining Social Support

Explain to participants the importance of letting people know the kind of support needed.

> *It is important to inform the people in your lives of the type of support that you require from them. You must also allow the support giver the opportunity to say no. This may not be a personal rejection but a statement of their inability to respond to the demand. This can be helped by making clear your request by specifying the extent and duration of support required.*

Use the example of asking a friend to take you shopping the next time he goes. It may be important to let the friend know that you need him to take you shopping only this one time because your spouse, who normally takes you, has his car in for repair.

Maintaining Social Support

Let group members know that support is an exhaustible resource, and if it is not taken care of or used wisely, it can become less helpful or disappear entirely. Participants should always acknowledge the help and support they receive from others. Also, participants should realize that the people who support them may need support themselves at times.

The Future

You may use the following sample dialogue to sum up the program:

> *It is hoped that the skills you've learned in this course will increase your ability to cope and manage your lives in the future. The next task for you all is to develop new life goals, continue working on those goals you've already established, and plan for your future.*

In this program we have attempted to highlight some of the coping skills that will help you maintain your psychological health. Research indicates that people with spinal cord injuries can obtain a level of life satisfaction at least as high as, if not greater than, their life satisfaction before the injury. We hope that as a result of participating in this program, you will be more aware of your stress and the techniques you can use to manage it, informed about helpful coping strategies, able to identify and reduce coping strategies that don't help, and able to deal with the consequences of your spinal cord injury and look to the future with optimism.

If you find yourself feeling down at some point in the future, refer back to the skills you have learned and practice them. The more you use these skills, the more effective you will become at managing any difficulties that may arise.

Close the session by asking the group for their feedback about the program.

Reference

Wycherley, B. (1987) The Living Skills Pack. East Sussex: South East Thames Regional Health Authority.

Fidelity Checklists

Session 1: Introduction to Stress and Coping

Fidelity Checklist

Date: _____

Therapist: _____

Group: _____

Rate your fidelity to each session element on a scale of 1 to 7, with 1 indicating poor fidelity and 7 indicating high fidelity.

Rating:

_____ Provide overview of program

_____ Make introductions

_____ Give practical information about group meetings (e.g., schedule, location, group rules, etc.)

_____ Define stress and stress reactions

_____ Discuss stress as it relates to spinal cord injury (SCI)

_____ Present the cognitive model of stress and coping

_____ Assign homework

Session 2: Assessing and Managing Stress

Fidelity Checklist

Date: _____

Therapist: _____

Group: _____

Rate your fidelity to each session element on a scale of 1 to 7, with 1 indicating poor fidelity and 7 indicating high fidelity.

Rating:

_____ Review previous session and homework

_____ Begin appraisal skills training

_____ Teach the group how to break down complex stressors into manageable parts

_____ Introduce the concept of coping

_____ Define adaptive coping

_____ Assign homework

Session 3: Problem Solving

Fidelity Checklist

Date: _____

Therapist: _____

Group: _____

Rate your fidelity to each session element on a scale of 1 to 7, with 1 indicating poor fidelity and 7 indicating high fidelity.

Rating:

_____ Review previous session and homework

_____ Introduce problem-solving method

_____ Provide group with examples of problem solving

_____ Assign homework

Session 4: Managing Emotions

Fidelity Checklist

Date: _____

Therapist: _____

Group: _____

Rate your fidelity to each session element on a scale of 1 to 7, with 1 indicating poor fidelity and 7 indicating high fidelity.

Rating:

_____ Review previous session and homework

_____ Present cognitive model of emotions

_____ Introduce pleasant activity scheduling as a way to combat negative thoughts

_____ Introduce autohypnotic relaxation technique

_____ Assign homework

Session 5: Changing Negative Thinking

Fidelity Checklist

Date: _____

Therapist: _____

Group: _____

Rate your fidelity to each session element on a scale of 1 to 7, with 1 indicating poor fidelity and 7 indicating high fidelity.

Rating:

_____ Review previous session and homework

_____ Discuss negative automatic thoughts and review common thinking errors

_____ Review steps for challenging negative thoughts

_____ Assign homework

Session 6: Maladaptive/Adaptive Coping

Fidelity Checklist

Date: _____

Therapist: _____

Group: _____

Rate your fidelity to each session element on a scale of 1 to 7, with 1 indicating poor fidelity and 7 indicating high fidelity.

Rating:

_____ Review previous session and homework

_____ Review general information about stress, appraisal, and coping

_____ Revisit coping strategies

_____ Discuss maladaptive coping

_____ Assign homework

Session 7: Social Support

Fidelity Checklist

Date: _____

Therapist: _____

Group: _____

Rate your fidelity to each session element on a scale of 1 to 7, with 1 indicating poor fidelity and 7 indicating high fidelity.

Rating:

_____ Review previous session and homework

_____ Discuss social skills and ways to deal with people without a disability

_____ Explain the importance of being assertive

_____ Introduce the concept of social support and the different types available

_____ Talk about ways of obtaining and maintaining social support

_____ End the program

References

Craig, A., Hancock, K., & Dickson, H. (1999). Improving the long-term adjustment of spinal cord injured persons. *Spinal Cord, 37*(5), 345–350.

Duff, J., & Kennedy, P. (2003). Chapter 14: Spinal cord injury. In S. Llewelyn, & P. Kennedy (Eds.), *Handbook of clinical health psychology* (pp. 251–278). Chichester: John Wiley and Son Ltd.

Elliott, T. R., & Kennedy, P. (2004). Treatment of depression following spinal cord injury: An evidence-based review. *Rehabilitation Psychology, 49*(2), 134–139.

Kennedy, P., Duff, J., Evans, M., & Beedie, A. (2003). Coping effectiveness training reduces depression and anxiety following traumatic spinal cord injuries. *British Journal of Clinical Psychology, 42*, 41–52.

Kennedy, P., Marsh, N., Lowe, R., Grey, N., Short, E., & Rogers, B. (2000). A longitudinal analysis of psychological impact and coping strategies following spinal cord injury. *British Journal of Health Psychology, 5*, 157–172.

Kennedy, P., & Rogers, B. A. (2000). Anxiety and depression after spinal cord injury: A longitudinal analysis. *Archives of Physical Medicine & Rehabilitation, 81*, 932–937.

Kennedy, P., Taylor, N. M., & Duff, J. (2005). Characteristics predicting effective outcomes after coping effectiveness training. *Journal of Clinical Psychology in Medical Settings, 12*(1), 93–98.

King, C., & Kennedy, P. (1999). Coping effectiveness training for people with spinal cord injury: Preliminary results of a controlled trial. *British Journal of Clinical Psychology, 38*, 5–14.

Lazarus, R. S., & Folkman, S. (1984). *Stress, appraisal and coping.* New York: Springer.

Martz, E., Livneh, H., Priebe, M., Wuermser, L. A., & Ottomanelli, L. (2005). Predictors of psychosocial adaptation among people with spinal cord injury or disorder. *Archives of Physical Medicine and Rehabilitation, 86* (6), 1182–1192.

Reidy, K., & Caplan, B. (1994). Causal factors in spinal cord injury: Patients' evolving perceptions and association with depression. *Archives of Physical Medicine and Rehabilitation, 75,* 837–842.

Reidy, K., Caplan, B., & Shawaryn, M. (1991). *Coping strategies following spinal cord injury: Accommodation to trauma and disability.* Paper presented at the 68th Annual Meeting of the American Congress of Rehabilitation Medicine, Washington.

Tirch, D. D., & Radnitz, C. L., (2000). Spinal cord injury. In C. L. Radnitz (Ed.). *Cognitive Behaviour Therapy for persons with disabilities.* New Jersey: Jason Ironson Inc.

About the Author

Paul Kennedy, DPhil, MSc, FBPsS, CPsychol, is Professor of Clinical Psychology at the University of Oxford, Academic Director of the Oxford Doctoral Course in Clinical Psychology, and Trust Head of Clinical Psychology based at the National Spinal Injuries Centre, Stoke Mandeville Hospital. He studied at the University of Ulster and Queens University, Belfast, and has worked in clinical health psychology since his graduation from clinical training in 1984. He has established clinical health psychology services in a number of areas.

Professor Kennedy is an active researcher with a broad portfolio of research on adjustment, coping, and physical rehabilitation. He has published over 80 scientific papers for peer reviewed journals, been a chapter contributor to many books, and co-edited/edited a number of books on clinical health psychology and physical disability. He serves on the editorial board of *the Journal of Clinical Psychology in Medical Settings*, *Rehabilitation Psychology*, and *Neurorehabilitation*. He was elected a fellow of the British Psychological Society in 1999, served on the Committee of the Division of Health Psychology, and was a Fellow of Harris Manchester College, University of Oxford, in 2001. He is founding chair of both the Multidisciplinary Association of Spinal Cord Injury Professionals (MASCIP) and the European Spinal Psychologists Association (ESPA). In 2002, he was awarded the Distinguished Service Award by the American Association of Spinal Cord Injury Psychologists and Social Workers, and in 2005, he was awarded a visiting fellowship to Australia by the New South Wales Government, Ministry of Science and Medical Research. In 2004, he was a winner of the Buckinghamshire Hospitals NHS Trust Staff Award in the Service Excellence category. He is an enthusiastic scientist-practitioner and enjoys the interplay between service provision, research, and training.